NOVEMBER 2020

CLARION CALL TO THE NATION

AWAKEN-AMERICA

DANGER CLOSE

GUY DIFFENBAUGH, D.D.

Unless noted, all direct scriptural quotations are from the King James Version, KJV of the Bible.

Every attempt has been made by the publisher to secure the appropriate permissions for materials used in this book. If there has been any oversight, we will be happy to rectify the situation and a written request should be made to the publisher.

NOVEMBER 2020: Clarion Call to the Nation Awaken America – Danger Close

ISBN-13: 9781948934091

**Falcon Publishing House LLC
4251 Monument Rd Suite 302
Jacksonville, FL 32225**

Copyright 2020 Doctor Guy Diffenbaugh. All rights reserved. No part of this publication may be reproduced, stored in a retrieval system, or transmitted in any form or by any means, electronic, electrical, chemical, mechanical, optical, recording photocopying, or otherwise, without the express written consent of the copyright owner. No reproduction is permitted and is unlawful according to the 1976 United States Copyright Act. Printed in the United States of America.

TABLE OF CONTENTS

Acknowledgements

Dedication.

Capitalization

Introduction

Chapter 1: How the Current Malaise Began   1

Chapter 2: Importance of 2020   13

Chapter 3: Consortium of Evil   39

Chapter 4: Meet Satan's Generals & Their Puppets   57

Chapter 5: The Wall Must Fall   91

Chapter 6: The Final Thrust From the Left.   103

Chapter 7: The Awakening Must Happen   157

Epilogue   179

Other Books by this Author   183

ACKNOWLEDGEMENTS

I give all glory to God for using me for His purpose in Jacksonville, Florida and in the nations, especially Africa. Jacksonville is a strategic epicenter for a powerful move of God through the United States of America and out to the nations. Jacksonville is the Tip of the Spear. We truly live in the most exciting era of history and we will see a providential move of the hand of God in our city of Jacksonville, this nation, and the nations of the world.

To the Nation of The United States of America, she is the Republic to which I have pledged my allegiance. From my lifetime oath as an Army Officer to support and defend her Constitution, to the Providential Purpose of Almighty God for which the nation was founded, I decree Come Kingdom of God – Will of God Happen!

To my incredible wife Dr. Lindy Diffenbaugh. She is personified by wisdom, strength, loyalty, and love. She is also called to nations and I can assure you she is a mighty partner, powerful Intercessor, and that there is no one I would rather be with than my friend, love, and mother of my five amazing children. She is a powerhouse for the King of Kings and a formidable force in His service.

**DEDICATED TO
PRESIDENT DONALD
TRUMP &
FIRST LADY MELANIA**

Never compromising, President Donald J. Trump and First Lady Melania, have sacrificed deeply and serve honorably our great Constitutional Republic. Despite unrelenting personal attacks and efforts at undermining the Office of POTUS, the Trumps have given selflessly to defend and preserve the Constitution and citizenry of our nation. God is on their side, and if you would but search the depths of your being you too would conclude that they are an extraordinary gift to our nation. May God continue to bless this couple and the United States of America.

CAPITALIZATION

Dr. Guy Diffenbaugh has taken *Author's Prerogative* in capitalizing certain words which are not usually capitalized according to standard grammatical practice. This is done for the purpose of clarity and emphasis. Reference to the Ecclesia/Church/Bride are capitalized because of her union with Deity through Jesus Christ. Ministry gifts of Ephesians 4:11, are capitalized and/or in bold for emphasis. Major Christian movements or events may be found capitalized and or in bold.

Scripture is capitalized when it refers to the entire Bible. Logos/Word/Graphe may be capitalized. Parts of scripture and or certain text may be capitalized, found italicized and /or in bold to emphasize points or concepts. Scripture is from the King James Version of the Bible unless otherwise noted.

INTRODUCTION

"It was the best of times, it was the worst of times, it was the age of wisdom, it was the age of foolishness, it was the epoch of belief, it was the epoch of incredulity, it was the season of Light, it was the season of Darkness, it was the spring of hope, it was the winter of despair..."[1]

To set the stage, this decade, the 2020's, is the greatest era of history and an amazing time to be alive on the earth. We are witnessing the greatest clash between The Kingdom of Light and that of darkness to date. The speed of information and ability of nations to bring destruction

---
[1] A Tale of Two Cities, Charles Dickens, 1859

within seconds is unparalleled. Though evil is nothing new, it has nevertheless reached a zenith to date and is growing exponentially in its effort to destroy creation and culture.

What is the significance of November 2020 and the United States of America? The answer is everything. The nations of the world look to America for leadership, strength, economic assistance and stability. The nation is being unraveled by four years of destructive evil perpetrated for no other reason than removal of a President that threatens dominion of a deep state and its leaders. Their sole purpose is self-preservation of power and wealth and they will stop at nothing to retain the same. They do not care about you and me, and if you think they do you are delusional at best.

It should be obvious that I support President Donald Trump. Much to some people's dismay, God also supports President Trump. I can boldly proclaim and absolutely state this because the sitting POTUS aligns with His providential purpose for this nation and invokes His name.

I am putting pen to paper not only because I love my country and want you to understand the dire circumstances in which we find ourselves, but because I am led of the Lord to proclaim the truth. Truth has become an obsolete concept these days unless one reads the Bible (God's Word is absolute truth) or digs deep into the history of the Republic. Both are pillars of truth, the two strongest sources of light which are targeted for destruction by Democratic Socialism. If liberty and freedom are important to you, I admonish you to not be found apathetic. Do your patriotic duty and cast your ballot on November 3, 2020. Every vote for the freedom, redeemed by the blood of Christ and the American Soldier is critical to the survival of our Republic. We fight – we win. Will you do your part?

My clarion call is to awaken patriots in our nation. The clarion was a medieval horn with a very clear sound. The call made by the clarion is difficult not to hear. Danger close is a military term used when incoming ordnance is going to explode on an enemy and the friendly forces are in near proximity to that enemy. Awaken as the enemy is on our threshold.

I hope you read this book and that it enlightens and strengthens your resolve. I speak blessings upon you as you are a critical piece of the Awakening of the Providential Purpose of the Republic.

CHAPTER 1
HOW THE CURRENT MALAISE BEGAN

Evil began a long time ago in a garden called Eden with the seduction of the first created beings, Adam and Eve. The fallen angel, Satan, caused the first couple to sin and has throughout history perpetuated evil through strategically orchestrated idolatry. If you are a Christian, your Bible explains all this. If you are of the opinion that this is myth, your faith will always be deficient/incomplete, and you will not be prepared for what is transpiring before your very eyes. If you don't believe in the God of the Bible, I encourage you to read and seek that you can develop a relationship with the only living God and spend eternity with Him.

Emmanuel – God with Us

Sin opened the door to evil for mankind and the perfect world which the Creator designed. But God so loved His creation that He sent His only Son, Jesus Christ to atone for sin and open eternal life to all that would believe (John 3:16 paraphrased). Jesus was the second Adam. The first Adam was made a living soul, the last Adam was made a quickening spirit (1 Corinthians 15:45). Although man returned to sin, grace was given by Christ's once and for all time atoning sacrifice. The grace avails to us today; we can repent and turn from our wicked ways.

John Cecil Rhodes

Evil has come in many manifestations since Jesus Christ's atonement 2020 years ago. Its current iteration began in South Africa with a British man named John Cecil Rhodes. He was an imperialist mining magnate acquiring diamond mines and attaining to political power. Thus, began the continuous rape of people and natural resources in my beloved Africa (beloved because I am called to the continent of Africa), which insidious behavior continues today on a larger scale by many nations. John Rhodes was a ruthless imperialist and white supremist with grand ideas of a one world government by Great Britain. Through the tenants of Free Masonry, Rhodes conceived a secret order and in 1891 Cecil Rhodes, William Stead, and Lords Escher, Rothschild, Salisbury, Rosebery and Milner drew up a plan for a secret society (the "Round Table") that aimed to bring all habitable parts of the world under their influence and control. Cecil Rhodes died in 1902 leaving his entire fortune to the Rothschilds.

Seeds of the One World Government/New World Order

Cecil Rhodes' Round Table is responsible for the cabal that is pushing for the one world government/New World Order, which is a clearly evil plan designed to destroy our liberty and impoverish the vast majority. In 1892 Baron Alphonse de Rothschild went to New York for secret talks at the headquarters of Standard Oil, owned by John D Rockefeller.

Cecil Rhodes' Round Table led to the founding in 1921 of both the United States based Council on Foreign Relations (CFR) and Chatham House in London. Bilderberg was founded in 1954, the Club of Rome in 1968 and the Trilateral Commission in 1973. All of these organizations are dedicated to global governance, and there is extensive overlap in terms of the principle players. The same forces created the United Nations.

The League of Nations was founded in 1920 by Woodrow Wilson and advised by Edward Mandell House, who had close links with John D. Rockefeller, Paul Warburg and J.P. Morgan, all of whom were connected to the Rothschilds. These elite men were part of the cabal that met secretly in 1910 at Jekyll Island, Georgia, to establish an anomaly, sort of a private corporation with supposed Federal participation. The Federal Reserve was established and set tyranny in motion for the United States of America. In 1913 President Woodrow Wilson signed the Federal Reserve Bill. Upon later reflection, this President wrote that he was a most unhappy man having unwittingly ruined his country.

The United Nations

In 1921 The Royal Institute of International Affairs (RIIA, now Chatham House) in London, and the Council on Foreign Relations (CFR) in New York were founded with the backing of financial cabal elites: J. P. Morgan, Bernard Baruch, Otto Kahn, Jacob Schiff, Paul Warburg, and John D. Rockefeller. The Presidential Advisory Committee on Post War Foreign Policy consisted of 14 members, of which 10 were members of the CFR. In 1945 the Committee designed and President

Roosevelt sold the United Nations to the 50 nations that came to the post-war San Francisco conference. The U.S. delegation included 47 CFR members such as John Foster Dulles and Nelson Rockefeller. John D. Rockefeller, Jr, donated $8 million to buy the Manhattan site for the UN headquarters. **The United Nations has always been the designated mechanism**

by which global governance by the wealthy elite is to be achieved.

The United States Senate approved the United Nations (UN), because it was assured by the State Department that the UN in no sense constituted a form of World Government and that neither the Senate nor the American people need be concerned that the United Nations or any of its agencies would interfere with the sovereignty of the United States or with the domestic affairs of the American People. It was only a short five years later, in testimony before the Senate Foreign Relations Committee, CFR member James Warburg stated: *'We shall have world government whether or not you like it –by conquest or consent'.*

Momentum Builds

The work goes on and new organizations have been founded dedicated to achieving a one-world government. In 1954 the CFR and the Bilderberg worked towards the creation of the European Union. In 1968, the Club of Rome and it's two sibling organizations, the Club of Madrid and the Club of Budapest, founded by David Rockefeller, entered the cause of promoting a globalist agenda. Their purpose was to create crisis, especially environmental, through which the world could be united under a one world government. Then in 1973 the Trilateral Commission, was founded by David Rockefeller to bring together high-ranking people, politicians and businessmen from the US, Western

Europe and Japan to plan one world government and activities serving a globalist agenda. Major sponsors include wealthy revolutionist George Soros and Bill Gates, who was/is involved in the UN's vaccination programs.

It is rather obvious that the exploitation of our culture through the environmentalist movement, the idea of biodiversity taking precedence over the needs of humanity, and above all the hugely successful global warming scare, created and overseen by David Rockefeller, allowed increased power to United Nations bureaucrats, and an ever-increasing role for corporate-owned non-government organizations.

Today in the USA

Fast forward to the current scenario with its ever-increasing evil, lawlessness, and anarchy. The degradation of our nation and world seems unfathomable, but awaken as it is happening with increasing speed. I can't stress enough the need for an awakening. We have all experienced a gradual numbing leading to acceptance of what we know is wrong. As I write today, the destruction of culture is in high gear. Satan and his colleagues are instilling fear through the media they control, the international cabal, the Deep State of America and other nations and their political puppets. Accusations abound of racism and there is an attempt to erase history.

It is time to awaken and take a stand for righteousness and our inheritance secured by Jesus Christ, the King of Kings and Lord of Lords. I know my future is secure regardless of what may happen, but the King wants me to bring the lost with me. Let's begin to explore the criticality of November 2020.

CHAPTER 2

IMPORTANCE OF 2020

So why all the hullabaloo over 2020? Quite simply 2020 marks what I consider the beginning of an unparalleled decade for harvest of souls in the Kingdom of God and criticality of the role played by the United States of America. Whether you view it from a Christian or secular stance, it matters not. Even the worldly secular view knows and has stated that there exists a new normal. I titled this book November 2020 because the election of the next POTUS in this coming month and year is the determining factor of life and freedom, not only in our nation but worldwide. This election represents the culmination of a long, very dark, and very ugly internal manifestation of evil and injustice unparalleled in the history of the Republic. The only way we can bring change is through intercession and the ballot box. Both are critical to our survival as a fathering nation and leader of the free world.

The Trump Card Played

President Donald Trump was elected against all odds in 2016, which was prophesied as far back as 2007. Satan, his Deep State minions, and puppets, smug in their assured Democratic Party victory, received a salvo from God and the patriots of this nation. Thus, began escalation of the dark war on the Republic. President Trump's adversaries, the demonic and demonically inspired leadership of the Democratic Party, mounted a fulltime effort to destroy the POTUS. The deceitful and illegal activity actually began pre-election and has exponentially grown darker. Please know that your tax dollars are supporting dark and illegal activity deep beneath the façade of childlike buffoonery, constant propaganda, and lies of the main-stream media to smear and destroy a godly man and gift to the Republic. God is obviously in control as no weapon formed against our President has prospered.

The Charade Must End

The nation has prospered under President Trump's leadership, even though he must at all times be vigilant to constant barrages of evil surrounding him and his amazing family. Actually, President Trump is a razor sharp and uniquely chosen instrument of God, able to take the heat and thrive. Imagine what could be done if he had bipartisan cooperation and did not have to constantly deal with unfounded accusations. Furthermore, imagine the progress we might see if the Legislative Branch were to do the work that we taxpayers pay for them to do, rather than mounting a malicious, fulltime, unfounded hate campaign. The smart thing for the citizenry to do would be to support President Trump in his vision of draining the "swamp" of those who undermine the goals and life of the Republic. We must rally behind President Trump and put an end to destruction of our nation.

An Appeal to Young People

Though I despise politics, if I were a bit younger, I would run for office. Because of my age, I unfortunately must physically battle with my pen and more importantly in the Spirit. That is fine, but there must be physical representatives of the people on the ground and actively engaged in battle with those that would destroy the Republic. Many in the Legislative Branch of the Federal government need to retire or be voted out by the process of the citizen electorate. They will not go out on their own as they are too drunk on power, greed and evil. There are many very smart younger Patriots in our United States that should consider politics as a career and some that could function in higher Federal office immediately. If Representative Cortez (AOC) and her "squad" can get elected, you young Patriot should be a shoe-in. I appeal to you young Patriot.

Give Me Liberty

Will Americans weigh the facts or believe the lies the media and their masters have perpetrated against President Trump? If you are not supportive of a fair election, free of cheating tactics such as multiple votes, uncontrollable mail ballots, the dead voting, etc., then you are complicit in the downfall of the Republic. If by this point, I have succeeded in retaining your readership I am grateful. If the truth has infuriated you such that you are ready to put this down, I pray that you may someday come to the truth which sets us free. Freedom is never free as it always comes at a price. If my lack of "political correctness" is disturbing, deal with it because it may be indicative that truth needs to speak into your bondage. American patriot, Patrick Henry stated in a speech before the second Virginia Convention, March 23, 1775: "Give me Liberty or give me death."

Freedom is Precious and Never Free

Many American Patriots have signed blank checks for their lives which have been cashed by our nation. My wife Dr. Lindy and I signed one of these and because we are Army Officers, our commissions are indefinite, and that check can be cashed as long as we are alive. Yes, I am an extremely passionate Patriot and intolerant of anyone desirous of destroying my nation and the freedoms we enjoy. Ponder the very powerful and applicable statement of President Ronald Reagan in an address given on Oct. 27, 1964: *"Freedom is never more than one generation away from extinction. We didn't pass it to our children in the bloodstream. It must be fought for, protected, and handed on for them to do the same, or one day we will spend our sunset years telling our children and our children's children what it was once like in the United States where men were free."*

Evil Exists Among Us and Covets Your Freedom

I also have a consuming passion for Jesus Christ and the nations He has called me to. Have you ever considered that our enemy, Satan, the perpetrator of everything evil, seeks to lie, steal, and destroy to accomplish his purpose? Because only God is omniscient, Satan was just as shocked as his minions when God played the Trump card saving us from a planned destruction. Have you considered that socialism has never worked? Do you realize that only the elite will enjoy the spoils resulting from the proposed socialist agenda of the Democratic

Party and that you will face poverty and enslavement if they prevail.

Evil has Many Faces

Have you considered that in the not too distant future the Sharia Law of Islam is a distinct possibility? Can you imagine females wearing burkas and mutilation of their clitoris, and many freedoms that we take for granted withdrawn? Now I am quite certain that many readers will say that Muslim people are peaceful; in fact, they are until they are a majority in a population and the radicalized leaders are in power. The ensuing radical Islamic ideology and leaderships enforcement of their understanding of the Koran, brings the advent of a virtually inescapable cultural shift. If you think it impossible, do the math (the average Muslim family size is 8) and continue to read as I will later explain the darkness of Islam. All of this is the insidious nature of evil. Is this scenario what you really desire? If you say no, get beyond your apathy and vote.

I Can't Tolerate or Condone Evil

"Dr. Guy, being a Man of God, don't you consider your statements harsh and improper for a Christian?" I say absolutely not; read your Bible. We are not instructed to kill infidels as Islam teaches, rather we are to establish Kingdom culture. Jesus ministered in love and truth but was never apathetic or weak. He was about the Father's business as we should be. The Apostle Paul tells us in 2 Corinthians 3:17 " the Lord is Spirit: and where the Spirit of the Lord is, there is liberty." Paul also states in Romans 12:17-19 that we should not repay evil, rather *live peaceably if possible*, with all men, for it is written 'vengeance is mine saith the Lord.' We are to stand fast to that which is dear to us and never surrender our God-given inheritance.

How Do We Live in This World?

God never fails even one of His promises. If you are His, then you know that you are in His hands. Jesus said they, meaning His disciples, are not of this world even as I am not of this world (John 17:16). We are here for His purpose. Paul states in Philippians 1:21 that to live is Christ and to die is gain. I have been at the precipice of death and can attest to the truths of which Paul speaks. This is the promise for Christ's own. He is with us and will never forsake us. Psalm 1 reminds us that the righteous are set apart from the wicked and the wicked will perish. As I am writing here, I envisioned the utter horror of the angel with the sickle in Revelation 14 as he sweeps through the earth harvesting the wicked to experience the wrath of God.

We change the playing field through intercession that invokes the intervention of God and His angels. We then stand unshakable in our most holy faith and witness the miraculous of the Almighty fight our battles. When you put these truths into perspective, with attainment of faith, you reach that peace that defies the world's understanding and you are able to stand through whatever befalls you.

Purpose

We are all given purpose and it is never too late to accomplish the same. I realized my own in my latter years, but God is faithful. God's people are a prophetic people. God speaks through His living Logos, Jesus, via Holy Spirit and the graphe Word, and through Holy Spirit today in what we refer to as Rhema. These are the ways we hear from Almighty God. Rhema gives fresh life to His people down to the personal revelation. It comes in varying forms but mostly through the prophetic. Being we are a prophetic people, created in His image and living in a spiritual world, we therefore, when redeemed and alive to Holy Spirit, are able to give and receive prophetic revelation. If you are in Him, you have precious promises and a destined purpose – ask for revelation of the same. Holy Spirit and fathering leadership give you the ability to discern the truth and timing.

My Purpose

I knew in my early childhood that I was called by God to ordained ministry. I did not have the tools until receiving Holy Spirit in 1986. Revelation was activated as well as the enemy. The enemy fought very hard to destroy every step toward my purpose. Satan still fights but to no avail. My faith has become so strong that Satan is now just a constant annoyance. Satan has given his best shots at destroying me, my family, my nation, and my destiny. I could write an unbelievable book on that alone, but if you are seriously pursuing your destiny in God you understand a lot of what I'm alluding to.

Application

Activation of purpose is accomplished in God's perfect timing. If you try to get ahead of Him, the consequences of a premature move can be costly and of diminished effectiveness. I had to wait thirty years. During that incubation I received the tools. Shortly after receiving Holy Spirit I got serious and began a long difficult journey. It was such a long thirty years that I begged God to not take me without fulfilling my destined purpose. He is faithful and began activation of all that was shown me so long ago. During Bible School, in 1989-1992 at Christ for the Nations (CFNI), He planted vision for Africa and gave me a new tool of the Seer form of the prophetic by giving me a spiritual father every bit as strong as his. His was Paul Cain.

Spiritual Catharsis

Being that my call is to the nations, activation started five years ago with the education I needed and the finding of an apostolic fathering leader to assist Holy Spirit in leadership. Fathering is critical in accomplishing purpose. Dr. Don Lynch, my fathering leader, has stood with me and inspired growth. Nations and fathering are two of many sharp instruments in his forte (note this word not only means expertise but also the strongest part of a sword). He encouraged my wife and me to be authors, which has become spiritual catharsis in itself. As the event facing our nation in

November draws closer the spiritual battle intensifies. I hadn't planned on sharing some fresh revelation here as I finalize to get this treatise out, but here goes.

Revelation #1

We know God is about nations (Psalm 2). He has raised up a triumvirate of executive leadership in the forerunner nations of The United States, Brazil, and Great Britain. These men are willing to take a stand for righteousness and freedom regardless of what the Deep State does. I knew that my beloved Africa had to be somehow involved and wondered how. August 8, 2020 provided my answer. I have seen visions and experienced manifestations of the same, ever since my involvement with the Continent of Africa. In the vision on this particular day I was shown how and why God connected me with a powerful Apostle in Arusha, Tanzania. God has given him apostolic blueprints for many African nations and other nations of the world. I in turn linked our vision with his and introduced Dr. Jonas to Dr. Lynch and now we all see and share in the vision. We are all in with Dr. Jonas Michael's vision and his is huge. The Lord impressed upon me that Dr. Jonas would become involved in leadership of his nation which is in fact happening. Tanzania's President serves God and is endowed with a backbone of steel. God's orchestration of events is amazing to the smallest detail and the probability of all interconnecting events is beyond reason. Tanzania sits in the center of the African continent and Arusha is where East Africa has chosen to meet for policy amongst the participant nations. In the conference on 8 August at Freedom House Jacksonville we were told that Apostle Clay Nash had a dream that it was time to move the Gerald Ford aircraft carrier from its Jacksonville assignment to the heartland where the Missouri River meets the Mississippi River. This is spiritual and not physical, but you will get it if you realize the reality of our living in a spiritual world. In a nutshell Apostle Dutch Sheets explained that Dr. Lynch ordered the carrier to the first coast of Jacksonville, where the Huguenots landed and prayed the first prayer in America. The dream and the various nexuses connecting the dots are in my book *Jacksonville: The Tip of the Spear*. Apostle Sheets saw God hovering over Jacksonville and the ancient gates opening. The big mission was launching screaming eagle intercessors to change the judiciary of our nation. The Gerald Ford is now moving to the heartland to speak in a larger way to the nation. In my vision concerning Africa, the heartland will speak also to the heartland of Africa in Tanzania and raise up leadership that will join the forerunner nations.

Revelation #2

Additionally, on August 8, 2020 I saw in the spirit the meaning and application an old prophecy from my CFNI sojourn. **The prophecy was to me, but today it speaks to Kingdom leadership in our times.** If it speaks to you, ask the Lord to so mantle you. I share the prophecy given me in our prophetic presbytery, October 28, 1993, by Pastor/Prophet Olen Griffing, upon our acceptance by Shady Grove Church's elders. *The Lord spoke to my heart that He has placed upon you a mantle of evangelism and that a deep desire to fulfill the commission of the Lord Jesus Christ is going to be released in a powerful way. And what I saw was a rally-man. I saw a man standing in the midst of a battlefield with a flag, with that banner lifted high. "And you're crying out: no, no, don't look at what the enemy is doing, the enemy has no power or authority over you." And I see you holding that ensign and you're a rally-man and an encourager and you're calling to the men "come around, we have not lost but we have won – don't listen to the enemy as the enemy has fallen."* *And I see you as a man who will proclaim words over the enemy. You will declare his destruction. You will declare it to other men. You will declare it to all ears. You will declare it into the air that the power of the enemy has been broken and I have created you, man of God as an authority, a man who will gather others around you, as a man who has a heart broken for other men. When you see men hurting, you hurt and you heal. And I'm putting in you the anointing to heal them.*

The Two Kingdoms

Contrast the ideologies, methodology of attainment, and results of Jesus Christ's Ecclesia with the kingdom which Satan has propagated. Both kingdoms must be fought for to attain and maintain, but the battles are different as well as the outcomes. Satanic dominated forces work through deception until the person submits to enslavement with failure to submit requiring imprisonment or death. The Ecclesia of Christ is exposition of truth and freedom obtained through intercession. The battle is spiritual and man's understanding of Christ's concept often misunderstood. Requisite of the Christian is spiritual battle, but when required we must physically stand our ground. "For our struggle is not against flesh and blood [contending only with physical opponents], but against the rulers, against the powers, against the world forces of this [present] darkness, against the spiritual *forces* of wickedness in the heavenly [supernatural] *places.* (Ephesians 6:12 Amplified Bible)

Ecclesia: God's Plan

So, what is God's plan? Quite simply the Ecclesia (Church),which lost its way toward the end of the first century and has become much like the world. Through many iterations we are beginning to resurrect Jesus Christ's design to establish Kingdom Culture, in order that He can establish His Ecclesia or government. It is happening; hence the horrific fight being waged by the kingdom of darkness. Satan knows his time is short and therefore his acceleration of evil and the intensity of those favoring his kingdom of darkness. It is really quite logical and happening before your very eyes.

America Hangs in the Balance

November 2020 and the fate of our nation, the United States of America, hangs in the balance. It is my fervent hope and belief that we will not have to endure more judgement, as in my opinion we did with two terms of President Barack Obama. I decree a second term for President Donald Trump and that the enemies of our nation will fall. Reformation will happen and the United States of America will continue in the providential purpose of Almighty God to be a beacon of light and hope to the world.

CHAPTER 3

CONSORTIUM OF EVIL

Significance of Jacksonville, Florida

In my book <u>Jacksonville – The Tip of the Spear</u>, I included the reasons why Jacksonville is so very significant in the current global scenario, as well as the major forces in what I believe to be the most significant and perhaps final end-time battle. Jacksonville, Florida, is an epicenter in the war and coming victory. It comes as no great surprise that events landed President Donald Trump's acceptance of nomination of his party coming from Jacksonville (recently cancelled because of the plannedemic of Covid-19). Perhaps you have heard eschatology all of your life and maybe even come to a conclusion as to what version seems most correct to you. Getting wrapped up in one version or the other is really irrelevant, because only Father God knows the scenario and time. Scripture gives us signs to look for and instructions as to how we should respond and live. The bottom line is that we are in a battle which gets more heated each day.

Why I'm Writing This Treatise?

The battle has been waged since the first Adam and will one day reach its final crescendo. I am of the opinion that there is not a lot of time remaining and hence the focus on harvest in the decade of the 2020's. I write from a spiritual standpoint because I realize that the spirit world is more real than that of the tangible world in which we live. I witness the power of the one true living God as well as that of darkness and can attest to the Victor. I write because I love my country and I love you. God does require me to love you, but there is no requirement to like you or what is transpiring in our nation and the nations of the world. My work is to eschew evil and proclaim the Gospel of Jesus Christ as long as I am present on the planet.

Our World Today has Accelerated

In my childhood we were not faced with the degree of evil our children face. My parents did not lock the doors to our home and we as children were free to roam the streets after school until the streetlights came on. Evil has grown exponentially in my frame of reference with a corresponding and significant decline in morality to the point that the envelope is pushed each and every day. Since becoming a Spirit filled Christian in 1986, I have been acutely aware of the enemy as well as the degradation of society.

Exponential Manifestation of Evil, Jerks Me into Reality

In the year 2008, I began to see my country exponentially unravel and real wickedness manifest in my nation. Though our nation has been controlled by a deep state and many self-serving politicians for many years, the election of Barack Obama as POTUS set in motion an unparalleled degradation of culture and emergence of evil. My nation has condoned evil and treason. I at least must call it out and through prayer and action do all that I am able to stand against the same. My real understanding of this ungodly leadership came in 2011 on vacation in Orlando, Florida, as I watched Glenn Beck on television. He walked his viewers though a diagram of President Obama's power structure which I am including for your examination. You should pay close attention to the key persons and follow the flow of money.

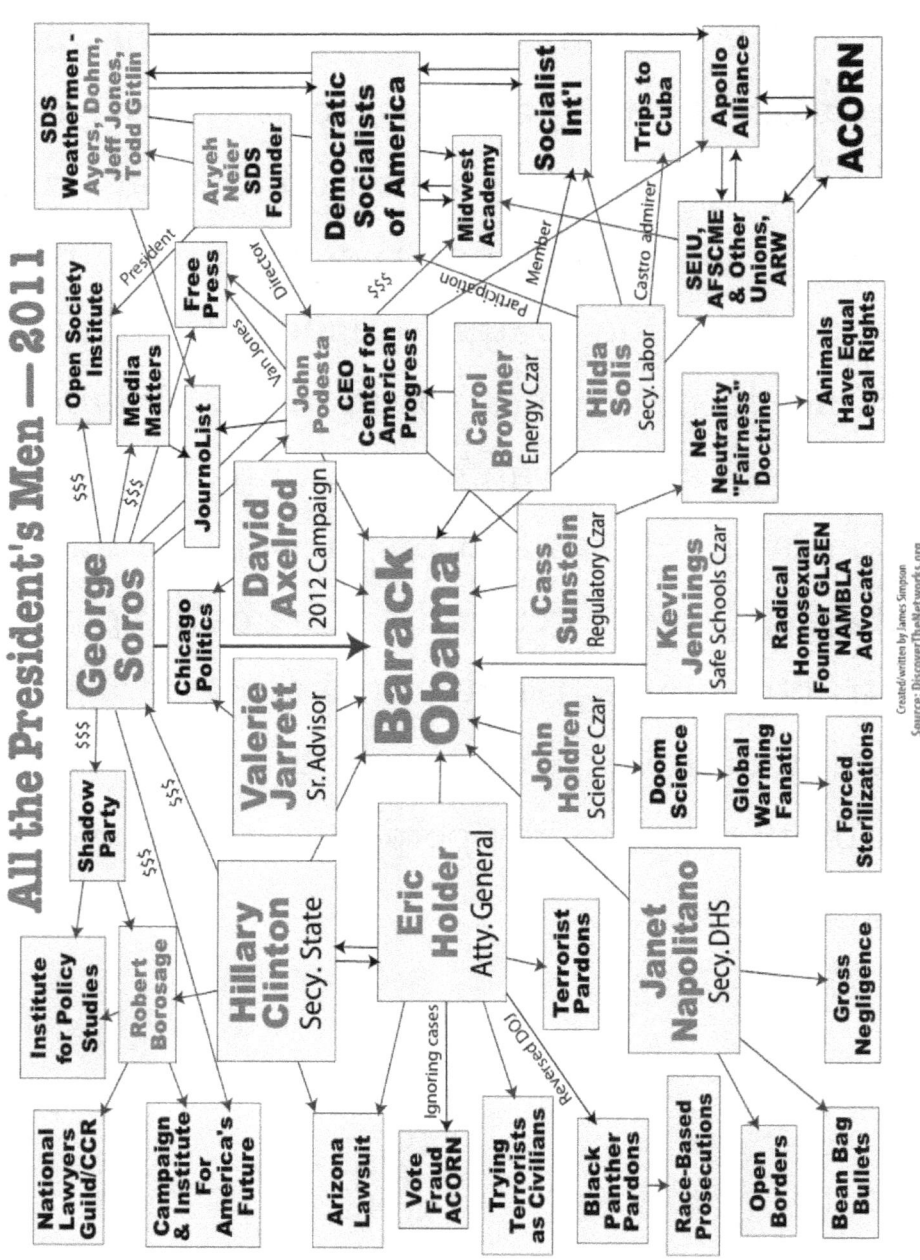

This chart can be found at http://www.libertygunrights.com/presidents-men-chart.pdf as well as a short explanation of players and organizations. The players are extreme socialists heavily indoctrinated in Communist theory. Their purpose is to destroy the United States by any means necessary, eradicate and rewrite her proud history, enslave the masses, and become powerful wealthy leadership in the New World Order (NWO) of the political/financial cabal led by Satan himself. Notice in the chart how the money flows and the presence of one of the higher-level members of the international cabal, George Soros.

Clarion Call for the Republic

I have made my purpose clear that I am writing to present the truth and awaken the good but apathetic and sometimes lazy Americans to the clear and present danger on the horizon. Get yourself and your sphere of influence ready for the emerging battle. The battle will always exist, but this time it represents life or death, blessings or curses. Politically, your ballot on November 3, 2020 will be the most important vote you have made in your lifetime. This is my clarion call for the preservation our Nation, the freedoms we enjoy and the providential purpose of Almighty God in and through the United States of America. God says choose life!

Foiled Plans of 2016

The NWO cabal through its network of "the deep state" that owns the spineless politicians of our nation was on a roll and was set to finalize the dismantling of the United States. They planned to accomplish this through the inevitable and expected 2016 victory enthroning Hilary Clinton as POTUS. Never did they consider the intervention of God playing the "Trump card" nor the resolve of quiet yet strong God-fearing patriots that made a statement. **It is time to make that statement again.** Recall my quoting earlier of President Ronald Reagan in an address given on Oct. 27, 1964 concerning freedom. We cannot and must not let this happen. Make sure that you cast a wise ballot on November 3, 2020, as it represents life or death of the Republic. If we fail, you will lose your freedom and the nation will become a similar entity to third-world nations. From there the reconstitution of that which has made us great will be an almost impossible and daunting at best task. Do you really want to go there?

Study Truth and Show Yourself Approved

It is so difficult to ascertain the real truth of anything these days, but if one searches and relentlessly fights, the lies will begin to crumble, and the truth will be exposed. Perhaps the biggest perpetration of fraud began with the sealing of documents concerning Barrack Obama. This was done in order to grease the skids for the One World Government (NWO) to establish a puppet in the United States of America, the last bastion of hope and freedom and stability for the world.

With the Democrat/Cabal ownership of most of the media, the ability of truth to surface was and is greatly hindered and suppressed. The issue of the very legitimacy of Obama's legal ability to even be POTUS was suppressed by media and fabricated documents concerning his birth. Having ministered in Kenya, I can assure you that Kenyans know Mr. Obama is a native son of that nation. Recently there has been a crack in the dam of obstruction and the Kenyan government has released eleven government documents: ***Nairobi: The Office of the Principal Register of the Nyanza Province, in Kenya, has finally released 11 exclusive documents concerning Barack Obama's alleged birth and early childhood in the***

country. *These official papers had been requested for many years by the Tea Party Patriots, a conservative American organization, to no avail, but the Kenyan Supreme Court recently ordered authorities to release the documents, based on a law on "access to information. These files, if they turn out to be verifiable, could mean that Mr. Obama had no legal right to become the American president under the country's law. The papers released today suggest that Barack Obama was actually born on March 7, 1960, in Lamu, Kenya, more than a year before his father moved to Hawaii, where he allegedly met his mother. This contradicts most of the documents presented by the presidential office over the last years, suggesting that* *either the American or the Kenya papers are actually faked.*[1]

Mass Deception

It is very hard to ascertain the truth without the Holy Spirit of God. This is precisely why I am compelled to present the inerrant truth from the living word of God. As I present a case against the enemies of the Republic, and the world for that matter, it must be presented within the construct of the righteousness of God upon which the founding fathers based the Constitution and moral direction of the United States of America. They always sought God before taking action. The United States must return to her principles as one nation

[1] https://worldnewsdailyreport.com/kenya-authorities-release-barack-obamas-real-birth-certificate/

under God; anything less will degradate and destroy the foundation and principles of our great nation. The veracity of information presented here, and yes, the Biblical truth which never falters, is conclusive evidence that many are being deceived by the god of this age, Satan, whose purpose is to destroy mankind. My hope is that I am able to assist in shattering all the lies perpetrated by Satan through the Democratic Left to establish darkness and death. Some within the United States Senate have finally acquired the intestinal fortitude to go after the truth and as I begin to finish this treatise, perpetrators of the lies and allegations against President Trump are surfacing. Hopefully the current Senate investigations and the work of US

Attorney John Durham's investigation, commissioned in May 2019 by Attorney General Bill Barr, will yield indictments and put an end to some of the Deep State evil.

The global probe was initiated to determine the veracity of Democratic Party allegations, pre-election and post-election, of supposed intervention with Russia to influence the Presidential election,

Exposure of the Dark Underbelly of the Deep State in America

We the People must come to a place of demanding justice. As is being consistently shown, the accusations of the Democratic Left are false allegations or "fake news" as the President calls it. We have been lied to so much that we come to expect it and even Republican law makers, some of which are complicit with the Deep State, live in fear of loss, retribution or both and are content with kicking the can down the road. When will we see imprisonment for perjury and death for treason rather than a slap on the wrist? We are beginning to see the exposure of evil and injustice. I hope our patriotic lawmakers don't succumb to threats of the Deep State and instead choose to stand their ground for America, as has our President. I also hope that John Durham's report comes before the election and yields many indictments.

As a man of God and an uncompromising patriot I cannot remain silent. Far too many of those who went before us have spilled their blood for you and me to have freedom. I stand for God and Country. How about you? Ponder the truth and act accordingly because tomorrow may be too late. The truth will set you free.

CHAPTER 4

MEET SATAN'S GENERALS

In Matthew's Gospel 10:6 Jesus warns us that He is sending us out like sheep among wolves and that we are to be wise as serpents and harmless as doves. The wolves are everywhere, even in the church. In the parable of the wheat and tares, Matthew 13:24-30, we see that the enemy planted tares amongst the wheat. The master did not uproot the wheat by pulling the tares. The two grow together and at harvest are separated and the tares burned. The parable indicates that evil will be amongst us as the wolves of Matthew 10:6. So good and evil must coexist on the earth until the day in which the Father designates that it is the final harvest.

Devil on a Mission

Since Satan rebelled against God and was expelled from heaven with a third of the angels that supported his rebellion, he has in his hatred sought to destroy mankind, which was created in God's image and destined to rule and reign with Jesus. Satan is determined to kill, steal, and destroy through a sophisticated hierarchy assembled to obtain his purpose. He has beguiled men and women since the beginning of their creation, especially those possessing or aspiring to power. These are most willing to take the bait and influence the decisions of the masses.

Satan's Primary Alliances with Man

It is my opinion that Satan has chosen the leadership of Islam and the Roman Catholic church to orchestrate his bidding. Though Islam is exponentially growing, it is the leadership of the Roman Catholic Church that has secured the power through alliances with the elite in politics, government structures, and wealth. Pope Francis is building alliances with the Islamic nations. If the preponderance of power and wealth resides with the Vatican and the Vatican is pursuing things abominable to God, it is quite easy to see the primary strategy of Satan and know our enemy more thoroughly. The leadership of both perpetrate and perpetuate evil and are adept at leading their following, many of which are unaware, into Satan's diabolical scheme. Islam seeks to destroy what they refer to as infidels. Their targets are Christians and Jews and the nations that represent the strongest threat to their agenda, the United States and Israel. Islam works through violence and terrorism and Rome through politics, deception, and wealth.

Islam

Islam is a key strategy of Satan that few Christians understand, but at the same time, it is critical that we do. *According to Kamal Saleem, a former Jihadist commissioned by the Muslim Brotherhood, the key message of Islam is jihad as a slave of Allah. Islam is more a political system than a religion. It is designed to deceive and establish an Islamic State (ISIS) that would usher in Ummah (one world order under Allah). The goal is to destroy the USA and Israel by the infiltration of all levels of society, through as many generations as necessary, warring against a nation's future, cursing its seed and everything of God. The attack on USA started in 1960. Islamists know we are in the end of days and their intent is to bring the great and final Iman who will call the antichrist to launch a war and destroy all Jews & Christians.*

The observance of Ramadan commemorates when Muhammad had a seizure and was demonized to be the satanic warlord, turned by Satan from peaceful to radical terrorism. At Ramadan Islamists ask Allah to fill them with the satanic spirits, a spirit of Legion which is the spirit of Islam, that possessed Muhammod.[1]

Islam Peaceful?

Have you ever seen peace in the Middle East? The answer is "no" because it has never existed and will only exist upon the return of the victorious King of Kings, Jesus Christ. The why is quite simply the tiny nation of Israel, established and given by God to a people of His choosing.

1 May 2019, Intercessors for America, https:www.youtube.com/watch?v=lmrxgf_AgVE

Depending upon one's spiritual orientation Israel is either hated or loved. This also represents the spiritual core of hatred toward the United States because she is protective of Israel. The relationship with Israel runs deep, and we must never forsake that relationship if we wish to remain blessed. From her inception the Republic has been blessed. The American Revolution was financed mostly by an unsung hero, a Jew named Haym Salomon. As Israel's principal ally, the United States is hated by Satan and his minions and marked for destruction. The declaration of President Donald Trump that Jerusalem is the capital of Israel and ordering the State Department to begin movement of our Embassy to Jerusalem sent shockwaves of hate throughout Satan's camp, especially his minions in Islam. Islam truly wants its final Iman to come and call the antichrist to arise and destroy Israel and the United States such that the Islamic State can spread its ideology of hatred throughout the world.

Rome

While everyone should be able to see the danger of Islam, Rome is a more subtle move of Satan. While Roman Catholicism is thought by many to be the true church directly tied to the Apostle Peter, it has a long history of evil leadership. I will spend more time with Rome because it is more complex, and its leadership is insidiously evil and powerful. I apologize in advance for offending many brothers and sisters in

Christ. Please know that I love and respect you and am only trying to expose the evil in leadership of the church that has deceived you and many.

Connection with New World Order

Governments, church, secret societies, and powerful people of greed are implementing Satan's diabolical plans in accelerated fashion because Satan's time is short. It is my opinion that Pope Francis is a chief proponent of a one world order or government. We see in the papal documents and in the papal thoughts, ideologies, and actions, a progressive and growing trend in leadership. As darkness is exposed to light withheld secrets manifest, dark secrets from many centuries past. In reading Pope Francis's Encyclical Letter

Laudato Si', he states in #175 that **"there is urgent need of a true world political authority**, as my predecessor John Paul XXIII indicated some years ago."[2]

In Pope Benedict XVI's Encyclical Letter Caritas in Vertate of 2009, # 146 he made the exact same statement that Francis later used "there is an urgent need of a true world political authority, as my predecessor Blessed John XXIII indicated some years ago."[3]

UN Agenda 2030 and Pope Francis

On the international scale the United Nations draconian 15-year plan, Agenda

---

[2] http://w2.vatican.va/content/francesco/en/encyclicals/documents/papa-francesco_20150524_enciclica-laudato-si.html

[3] http://w2.vatican.va/content/benedict- xvi/en/encyclicals/documents/hf_ben- xvi_enc_20090629_caritas-in-veritate.htm

2030 (its implementation date), is merely a plan for a global government tyranny. The obvious enslaving coercion is One World Government. The September 25, 2015 keynote speech before adoption of the resolution was given by none other than Pope Francis, whom I believe to be its major proponent. The agenda never mentions God or protection of the rights given by Him as the Creator. It is point by point a socialist agenda which, coincidentally, mimics the socialist agenda of the radical left that is so intent on destroying the constitutional republic of the United States of America. UN Agenda 2030 is tyranny and it is antichrist.

Blasphemous Proponent/Leadership of the UN?

It is important to note what Pope Francis said in that 2015 keynote speech before the United Nations. Twice, Pope Francis said: **"I come in my own name and that of the entire Catholic community."** In the fifth chapter of the Gospel of John, Jesus speaks of the difference between the true representative of God on Earth, Himself, and the Satanically produced counterfeit of the Antichrist and the False Prophet. In John 5:43, Jesus speaks the following astounding, prophetic words: "I am come in my Father's name, and ye receive me not: **if another shall come in his own name, him ye will receive**." Pope Francis says he comes in his own name.

One should question why he doesn't come in the name of Jesus or as the Vicar of Christ. Later, within this chapter, I will present the official meaning of "Vicar of Christ," as defined by leadership of the Roman Catholic Church. Essentially, they view the Pope and Christ as one and that any title given Christ can be applied to the Pope, which scripturally is idolatry and blasphemy. This would cause the reasonable man to question how he ends his speech with the words: "Upon all of you, and the peoples you represent, **I invoke the blessing of the Most High**, and all peace and prosperity." To which "most high" was the Pope referring? Satan the counterfeit, proclaims: "I will ascend above the heights of the clouds; I will be like the Most High." (Isaiah 14:14). [4]

A Voice for One World Government

Pope Francis continues to become more and more political and as reported on June 27, 2017, Pope Francis called for A ONE WORLD GOVERNMENT and *political authority* this week, arguing that the creation of the one world government is needed to combat major issues such as *climate change*. Speaking with Ecuador's El Universo newspaper, **the Pope said that the United Nations doesn't have enough power and must be granted full governmental control *FOR THE GOOD OF HUMANITY.*** *His appeal echoed that of*

[4] https://holyseemission.org/contents/statements/statements-56054736193b87.20279259.ph

his predecessor, pope benedict xvi, who in a 2009 encyclical proposed a kind of Super-UN to deal with the world's economic problems and injustices. David Rockefeller famously said that a *global crisis* would have to occur before the people of the world would be willing to accept a New World Order. The world religious leaders came together on June 14, 2017 to make a joint statement through a video calling on people to embrace ideas of friendship and unity, and to overcome negativity and division in society. In reality, the call for global government by Pope Francis and other wealthy elitists has nothing to do with lifting up impoverished nations or *saving humanity*. Such a government would instead guarantee global wealth inequality, surveillance, and a world run by the exact corrupt interests currently consolidating wealth and power worldwide."[5]

Fishing for Power in Islam's Pond

On 4 February 2019, in Abu Dhabi, Pope Francis and the Grand Imam of Al-Azhar, Ahmad Al-Tayyeb, signed a historic covenant between Roman Catholics and Islam called Human Fraternity for World Peace and Living Together. Within a paragraph about human freedom, the document states that religious plurality is willed by God. "The pluralism and the diversity of religions, color, sex, race and

---

[5] https://prophecyinthenews.com/world_news/pope-francis-calls-for-one-world- government- to-save-humanity/

language are willed by God in His wisdom, through which He created human beings."6

Pope on Pedophilia and Sexual Abuse

Regarding the sexual abuse and pedophilia within the Roman Catholic opinion entitled <u>The Strange Disconnect between Pope Francis' Words and Actions about Sex Abuse</u> are the following excerpts. In an address to bishops in in Philadelphia, Pope Francis said: "The crimes and sins of sexual abuse of minors cannot be kept secret any longer. I commit myself to the zealous watchfulness of the church to protect minors, and I promise that all of those responsible will be held accountable.

6 https://www.catholicworldreport.com/2019/02/04/pope-francis-signs-peace-declaration-on-human- fraternity-with-grand-imam/

The Pope's Corporate Veil

The maintenance of secrecy for these crimes is imposed by Article 25 of Pope John Paul's *motu proprio, Sacramentorum Sanc-titatis Tutela* of 2001, and by Article 30 of its revision by Pope Benedict XVI in 2010. These rules impose the pontifical secret on all allegations and proceedings relating to child sexual abuse by clerics. The footnotes to Article 25 and Article 30 apply. Article 1(4) of Pope Paul VI's instruction, *SECRETA CONTINERE*, which defines the pontifical secret as the church's highest form of secrecy, and like the secret of the confessional, is a permanent silence. Since becoming pope March 13, 2013, Pope Francis has made no attempt to change this maintenance of secrecy, the very thing he condemned in Philadelphia. On Jan. 31, 2014, the United Nations Committee on the Rights of the Child requested the Holy See to abolish the pontifical secret over allegations of child sexual abuse by clergy and to impose mandatory reporting. On May 22, 2014, the United Nations Committee against Torture requested the same thing. On Sept. 26, 2014, the Vatican responded and rejected these requests, stating that mandatory reporting under canon law would interfere with the sovereignty of independent nations.

In matters of child sexual abuse, Pope Francis has no Constitution, no Congress, no Senate and no Supreme Court that could restrain him from changing canon law. He has no obligation even to consult anyone. He is the last of the absolute monarchs. The buck for maintaining secrecy over the sexual abuse of children within the Roman Catholic Church truly stops with Pope Francis." [7]

The Pope and Masonry

There is a proliferation of literature surrounding the current Pope. When Francis was chosen Pope, he received congratulations from all over the masonic world. The masonic is a secret order and like the Vatican it is difficult to determine the truth. Conspiracy theorists believe

[7] https://www.ncronline.org/news/accountability/strange-disconnect-between-pope-francis-words-and-actions-about-sex-abuse, Kieran Tapsell, October 1, 2015

that the Jesuits, of which Pope Francis is one, exercise control of the masonic and the illuminati. It is understandable assumptions could be made very easily in this case. Why would the masonic embrace his papacy?

A Very Long History of Controversy

I don't know the depth of involvement or intent of the Roman Catholic Church in these last days, but I must state that what I see is not healthy and will not align with scripture. A wise teacher in Bible School at Christ for the Nations Institute said: "the truth usually lies somewhere between the two extremes." In sorting through a plethora of information concerning the beliefs and doctrines of the Roman Catholic Church, I believe the leadership is the issue. Even if there were only an ounce of truth in any accusation against that leadership it would still remain an abomination in the eyes of God. I will present one of many beliefs in the preeminence and regarded stature of the Pope as equal to the Godhead: **Dominum Deum Nostrum Papam - Our Lord God the Pope.**

In the official 1582 edition of Catholic Canon Law, we find the text of a papal bull that is the subject of much controversy, even among Catholics themselves, as many consider it to be an infallible magisterial pronouncement: Therefore, of the one and only Church there is one body and one head, not two heads like a monster; that is, Christ and the Vicar of

Christ, Peter and the successor of Peter, ... Therefore, whoever resists this power thus ordained by God, resists the ordinance of God [Rom 13:2], unless he invents, like Manicheus two beginnings, which is false and judged by us heretical, since according to the testimony of Moses, it is not in the beginnings but in the beginning that God created heaven and earth [Gen 1:1]. *Furthermore, we declare, we proclaim, we define that it is absolutely necessary for salvation that every human creature be subject to the Roman Pontiff.*

Blasphemy Because Only Holy Spirit is God Residing with Man

In the gloss by French canonist Petrus Bertrandus (Peter Bertrand 1280-1349) for the last sentence of Unam Sanctam, we find this: Christ entrusted his office to the chief Pontiff; (Mat 16:18, Mat 24:45) but all power in heaven and in earth had been given to Christ; (Mat. 28:18) therefore the chief Pontiff, who is His vicar, will have this power. **So, Christ and the Pope are a single head.** This sentiment is the same as that expressed in Our Lord God the Pope. (This hyperbole, as some would deem it, that easily crosses the line to blasphemy, is not uncommon among some Catholics).

Cardinal Robert Bellarmine (1542-1621), a Doctor of the Church, in his *Disputationes de controversiis christianae fidei, Adversus hujus temporis Haereticos (Debates on the Christian*

Controversies of Faith Against Contemporary Heresy), claimed that **all the names that Scripture applies to Christ are also to be applied to the Pope.**

Now that I have established my theory of Satan's primary demonized leadership, which he has designated to serve his purpose through man, we can move to his puppets. They are worldwide but the focus of this book is the United States of America.

Deep State and the Puppets

The monetary wealth of the international cabal, which I discussed earlier, is being used to manipulate world events and buy the media as well as many of the leaders worldwide and in the United

States. Once the hook is set it becomes very difficult to dislodge it and most decide, that having made the mistake, be it intentionally or unintentionally, they might as well enjoy the rewards of power and wealth. At this point Satan has won and there is not much chance of escape. The deep state refers to the embedded power of certain government leaders and employees, the military/industrial base, private corporate giants and foundations, and the financial elites of the world, whose lives are mired in darkness pursing power, wealth, manipulating and controlling those that make the laws, the purposes of which are those of their leader Satan. Almost all of those I have mentioned here are intoxicated to the point of no return and will do anything to retain their positions of power and wealth.

Where the Rubber Meets the Road

President Donald Trump is determined to usher in justice and drain the swamp of deep state operatives and their political pawns that seek destruction of the Republic. This is why the battle is so fierce in the United States. This is why the left will do anything to get the sitting POTUS out of office because their sycophantic, self-serving privileged lives are at stake.

The Puppets

I thought about calling these people out, but you know who they are. If you can seriously say that leaders such as Nancy Pelosi, Chuck Schumer, Adam

Schiff, Jerry Nadler, etc., as well as behind the scenes prospective or past leaders such as Joe Biden, Barrack Obama, and Hilary Clinton are in any way representative of the America men and women that patriots have fought and died for, then you are complicit in the destruction of this nation and don't deserve the privilege of living here. I love you and pray for you, but I don't like you if you espouse or believe in destruction of our nation which was conceived in God's name and providential purpose and protected by the blood of Patriots since its inception.

These Democratic Left leaders are not the sharpest crayons in the box, individually or collectively, and present to the be harmless servants fighting for you and for equality and justice. In actuality they are vipers that cozy-up to you and make promises that they never intend to keep, all of which is done to keep their position of power. The mean-spirited Democratic Party politicians almost total focus for four years, using your taxpayer dollars, has been to annihilate President Trump. Their hate grows exponentially, and they are consumed with the same. These are the law maker puppets remaining in office through intentional deceit, media propaganda, and the dark underbelly of their masters. The smoke and mirrors, as well as the creation of constant diversions to blame shift and divert focus off their evil agenda, is their modus operandi.

Who's Really in Charge?

Beneath this lawmaking face lies a web of almost impenetrable darkness labeled "Deep State." This is where sleuthing becomes a real chore until they make a mistake that surfaces and is sufficient enough to draw attention. Those cabal operatives somehow get swept under the rug, disappear, or seem to commit suicide in some most interesting ways, never making it to trial or deposition. The most notorious of these seem to be individuals whose testimony would destroy or bring serious trouble to the Clintons. It is speculated that the protection element, widely referred to as "The Clinton Crime

Cartel" have fifty plus deaths attributable to their work. Those that can cause them harm have lost their lives and it seems almost all are attributed to suicide. The big question would be how many have desired to spill the beans, but knew it would cost their life if it were even possible to get to testimony?

Echelons of Evil Will Meet Defeat

With each ascending level of leadership in the cabal, the power, money and protection render accessibility virtually impossible. This is the face of evil today. It is entrenched in very organized echelons and without God on our side we would perish. We have precious promises which cannot fail, and we will win because He says so. Christians awaken and realize your purpose. The Apostle Paul, in 2 Corinthians 4:7 says "we have this treasure in earthen vessels, that the excellency of the power may be of God, and not of us." Let God arise in you and me. Enlist today for the battle or at least vote in the 2020 Presidential election, as it is your duty as a citizen of this great nation.

Open Your Eyes and Engage Your Brain

I adjure you to examine the purpose which leaders on the Left are desperately pursuing and see through the veil of deception. Upon seeking the truth through serious study, thought, and prayer, I am convinced you will see the lies and that the Left is after personal gain, self-preservation and saving of their golden trough at your expense. If you refuse to see their hatred, deception, deceitfulness, treason and evil, this treatise is probably not for you and you must be loosed to your own recognizance.

Repent, Seek Wisdom, Walk in Righteousness

Solomon, King David's son, perhaps the wisest man in history wrote in Proverbs 14:34 "Righteousness exalteth a nation: but sin is a reproach to any people." Take a moment of reflection and most readers will know that their parents taught them right from wrong. Many have read or heard the Bible and if not, most know the truth. Take off the blinders, be accountable and hold your elected officials to the same measure. There is no excuse for not casting your ballot on or before November 3, 2020 and no excuse for not exercising wisdom.

CHAPTER 5

THE WALL MUST FALL

Walls are designed to protect as well as demarcate and limit. In Joshua Chapter 6 is found the scripture pertaining to the wall around the city of Jericho, which was the Israelites first battle in the conquest of Canaan. God instructed His people to walk around the wall seven times and then blow the shofar. They did as they were instructed, and God caused the wall to fall allowing for destruction of the enemy.

President Reagan stood at the Brandenburg Gate in West Germany on June 12, 1987 and gave his famous speech imploring Communist leader Mikhail Gorbachev of the Soviet Union to tear down the Berlin wall. *Behind me stands a wall that encircles the free sectors of this city, part of a vast system of barriers that divides the entire continent of Europe. . . . Standing before the Brandenburg Gate, every man is a German, separated from his fellow men. Every man is a Berliner, forced to look upon a scar. . . . As long as this gate is closed, as long as this scar of a wall is permitted to stand, it is not the German question alone that remains open, but the question of freedom for all mankind. General Secretary Gorbachev, if you seek peace, if you seek prosperity for the Soviet Union and Eastern Europe, if you seek liberalization, come here to this gate. Mr. Gorbachev, open this gate! Mr. Gorbachev, tear down this wall!*

I realize that I have quoted President Ronald Reagan often, but it is because this President had a keen assessment of the issues of his time and how they could affect the future course of the United States.

Walls and gates have always been important in the physical, but they are also extremely important in the spiritual realm. The Kings issued proclamations from the city gates. I proclaim the reign of the King of Kings and His Ecclesia from the spiritual gate of my city. I won't elaborate here but Holy Spirit will if you ask Him and you will receive a wealth of information and blessing.

Spiritual Walls Must Come Down

We all know what physical walls are, but far deeper and much more important are spiritual walls. If you are a Christian, Jesus Christ's most passionate intercession with His Father, the greatest prayer ever prayed, is in John 17. In verse 11 we see His desire that we be one: "And now I am no more in the world, but these are in the world, and I come to thee. Holy Father, keep through thine own name those whom thou hast given me, that they may be one, as we are." I present Ephesians 2 in its entirety as it is important to see the purpose of God as well as a contrast with the destructive agenda of Satan who is manipulating the world to destroy man, who is God's greatest creation.

Ephesians 2 (Passion Translation): *1As for you, you were dead in your transgressions and sins, 2 in which you used to live when you followed the ways of this world and of the ruler of the kingdom of the air, the spirit who is now at work in those who are disobedient. 3All of us also lived among them at one time, gratifying the cravings of our flesh and following its desires and thoughts. Like the rest, we were by nature deserving of wrath. 4 But because of his great love for us, God, who is rich in mercy, 5 made us alive with Christ even when we were dead in transgressions—it is by grace you have been saved. 6And God raised us up with Christ and seated us with him in the heavenly realms in Christ Jesus, 7in order that in the coming ages he might show the incomparable riches of his grace, expressed in his kindness to us in Christ Jesus. 8 For it is by grace you have been saved, through faith—and this is not from yourselves, it is the gift of God 9 not by works, so that no one can boast. 10For we are God's handiwork, created in Christ Jesus to do good works, which God prepared in advance for us to do. 11Therefore, remember that formerly you who are Gentiles by birth and called "uncircumcised" by those who call themselves "the circumcision" (which is done in the body by human hands) 12 remember that at that time you were separate from Christ, excluded from citizenship in Israel and foreigners to the covenants of the promise, without hope and without God in the world. 13But now in Christ Jesus you who once were far away have been brought near by the blood of Christ. 14For he himself is our peace, who has made the two groups one and has destroyed the barrier, the dividing wall of hostility, 15by setting aside in his flesh the law with its commands and regulations. His purpose was to create in himself one new humanity out of the two, thus making peace, 16and in one body to reconcile both of them to God through the cross, by which he put to death their hostility. 17He came and preached peace to you who were far away and peace to those who were near. 18For through him we both have access to the Father by one Spirit.*

19Consequently, you are no longer foreigners and strangers, but fellow citizens with God's people and also members of his household, 20built on the foundation of the apostles and prophets, with Christ Jesus himself as the chief cornerstone. 21In him the whole building is joined together and rises to become a holy temple in the Lord. 22And in him you too are being built together to become a dwelling in which God lives by his Spirit.

One New Man

Ephesians 2:14 speaks of Jesus Christ tearing down the spiritual wall of hostility between Jew and Gentile, which can also mean world, and verse 15 establishing "one new man." Christ's own are seated with Him in Heavenly realms, verse 6, that we be empowered and equipped to show forth His glorious plan in this world. Some will never see or understand His purpose and His promises, which are for now and in eternity, for which He allowed Himself to be a sacrifice for all men. The gate to life is open to all, but we are told by Jesus that it and the path are narrow. Our sacrifice yields a life of peace with all needs met "according to His riches in Christ Jesus."(Philippians 4:19). I implore you to take to heart Ephesians 2:22 and as we grow together by the Spirit of God within us, we will understand the absolute necessity of the liberty in Him and recognize the dark deceit of Satan as he seeks to destroy us.

Christian – Get it Right

Christians are perhaps their own worst enemy. Time is of the essence and it is time to acquire a backbone of steel. We must live in the world but not partake of the evil therein; in other words, "quit drinking the Devil's cool aid " and store some of your treasure in Heaven. We should not be hiding in church seeking solace as we wait for passage to our eternal reward.

Have you read your Bible? What does Jesus command you to do? The world already hates you as it did Him. The promise of eternity and all the attenuating joy is not promised for this life on planet earth. It is going to get worse even as the Lord promised. We are at war every day and really need you to actively fight with us. I can promise you that all you hold dear will be lost much quicker if you live in apathy and delusion. I can personally tell you that death is nothing to fear as I have been at its precipice. Fear is the antithesis of faith.

Christian Leader Awaken

I admonish all Christian minsters of the Gospel that are involved in building your own empires to repent and turn from the worldly trappings. No one should begrudge you a prosperous life, but if you are complicit with the world you surely know what judgement awaits you for failed leadership of those God has entrusted to you. Repent remains the word of the Lord throughout the ages. Join the battle; fight and win.

CHAPTER 6

THE FINAL THRUST FROM THE LEFT

As I write here in July 2020 it is difficult to imagine a more precarious situation for the nation of the United States of America, than the one we are witnessing. I do believe that a desperate deep state and their far-left puppets, which have ascended to positions of power and authority, are like hungry sharks that sense they might not feast on their ill-gained delicacies much longer. Possible loss of power, their life of greed, and the present and potential full unveiling of their evil schemes and illegal conduct have put them in a frenzy. They are consumed with protecting themselves at any cost and willing to perpetrate anything to destroy the current POTUS.

Ruse of the Plannedemic

The recent ruse of a "plannedemic", Covid19, orchestrated to destroy the POTUS and take the heat off the cabals own criminal activity at the cost of destruction of world economies, is appalling and insidiously evil. The hype of the media has assisted in making a virus seemingly more real than major viral diseases we normally face. I am not denying that Covid-19 is real, rather I am saying that the truth will surface and confirm what I am stating. I proffer to you that this is diversionary, and it is part of a sequential plan to beat you down mentally, physically and spiritually. Through induced fear, panic, violence, financial need, and the aforementioned 3 areas of destruction, the Democratic Socialists purposed agenda of government dependence and submission unfolds. The next step will be the vaccine containing the chip to track and control you, deceitfully initiated as needed to control the virus. Science and artificial intelligence have reached a level that a chip can take control of your brain. If this scenario were possible, and I believe it is, the Deep State might not even need a victory in November to take away your constitutional right to bear arms. If and when this scenario is played out, you are helpless and a victim to an insidiously evil plan from the pit of hell.

Dark Purpose of Engineering the Plannedemic Covid-19

As the dust begins to settle clues are beginning to emerge and it will eventually become apparent that orchestrated evil at high levels has been perpetrated. China, the developer has always been masters of deception. China produced one of the greatest strategists of all time Sun Tzu. Around 500 BC, Sun Tzu produced a classic called *The Art of War* containing timeless military principles such as "All warfare is based on deception" and "In the midst of chaos, there is also opportunity." It is readily apparent upon even causal observation that China is intent on world domination. Who could be a more sinister partner than a greedy secretive communist run nation. High level operatives of the cabal seized the opportunity because the incompetent and faltering Democratic Left couldn't destroy President Donald Trump. As long as President Trump remained in office, the cabal's plan to implode the United States would be impossible. Covid-19 would start a last-ditch effort to remove President Trump at all costs.

Covid-Covert Dark Plan #1

The Cabal commissions its higher-level operatives to use China to birth the virus. It is rather ominous when we observe Bill Gates retiring from his software empire to ensure that the entire world will get a Covid-19 virus vaccination. Even darker and more sinister is the intent to place a microchip in the injection that will "track" the disease. It should be obvious that the chip is to monitor everything you do and thus enable the cabal to track you. My wife, Dr. Lindy, and I minister in Africa and the Africans don't trust Bill Gates because of the heavy death tolls which they attribute to his past vaccinations.

Covid-Covert Dark Plan #2

Much to my despair, as I write here, the success of the "A team" has probably even surprised their own expectations. They have put the world in a tailspin and the media has wielded lies and fear tactics masterfully.

Businesses are failing and employees are suffering. Most tragic of all, many are falling for the ruse and are being conditioned to fall into submission to "Big Brother." We are required to wear a face mask in public, even though the wearing of a mask causes hypercapnia; which is the level of CO_2 that builds up behind masks and rises in seconds from 400 ppm to 10,000+ ppm (parts per million). When we rebreathe our own CO_2, we reduce oxygen levels, causing increased respiratory and heart rate upsurge, leading to dizziness, faintness, brain fog, panic, increased cortisol levels. These results decrease our immunity. They also cause hypercortisolism. In a nutshell summary, masks reduce intake of oxygen.

In short; masks significantly reduce the amount of oxygen intake and cause driven out carbon dioxide to be breathed back in. The resultant respiratory damage is then labelled Covid-19 to pad the numbers creating usable false evidence and exacerbating the fear levels. All part of the larger plan to control or destroy dissidents. There is a substantial body of reliable scientific information and reports showing that the effectiveness of the very best surgical face masks is insufficient to provide enough protection for the wearer against COVID infections!

The public is being conditioned to blindly accept tyranny and dependence upon government to meet needs that were once earned through honest work.

Covid-Covert Dark Plan #3

Meanwhile behind the Covid smokescreen in America, the deceitful Democrat Left is plotting their presumed victory and the demise of capitalism in America, as well as their rise to power at the expense of our freedom. Speaker of the House, Nancy Pelosi, is again, as I write, attempting to legislate a cashless economy with complete control delegated to the Federal Reserve. Have you noticed that during the plannedemic many institutions no longer accept cash as it is "dirty" and a threat to employees. Right! The purpose is to move people from cash to electronic currency. The

Fed will be able to access and bleed your accounts at any time. Where the Left desires to go after this I don't know, but their master, Satan, does and it can only be destruction.

Digital currency, known as block-chain or crypto, such as Bitcoin, could be a good thing, because governments have no way to track it. On the other hand, the use of electronic currency administered by governments will take us straight into the tyrannous trap of the Deep State's financial cabal. I believe the abolishment of fiat currency and return to a gold backed standard, with President Trump leading the charge, is the nightmare to the cabal and another reason for pushing for electronic currency. President Trump also seems favorable to GESARA and NESARA, which are global and national financial resets. This is like the Jubilee in scripture which erases debts. The Deep State will fight to the death on this one because the results will wipe out their usurious and unethically obtained fortunes. I am not writing this financial information from deep knowledge of the system, but rather from what God is showing me.

I decree that America will awaken and forsake evil, repent, and return to their God given purpose and destiny and those who persist in evil and destruction will fall.

Anarchy

The unrest and pain of Covid-19 is being followed by violence which the left is incorrectly labeling racism, a convenient often played card. Let's call it what it really is – anarchy. After instilling fear of Covid-19 and isolating you, the next step is an attempt erase the history of our great nation and instill violence, denigrating all that we have held sacred. The death of George Floyd was a travesty, but most are unaware of the truth. It is known that he had substances in his body that are known to make one uncontrollable and his record as a citizen was far less than sterling. I watched one of the many memorial services orchestrated by the Reverend Al Sharpton, at best a fraud in Christendom, where the preponderance of the memorial was used to recognize and laud Sharpton's cronies involved in creating a hype in black Americans. Planned or unplanned the death of George Floyd was the perfect fuse for Black Lives Matter and Antifa to initiate civil unrest throughout the nation.

Behind the Scenes

Most of the Democratic Left are light years behind their opposition, Donald Trump, in intelligence, but have been very effective in getting what they want. The explanation can be ascertained from examination of their playbooks and realization that no matter how absurd or stupid something might be, if it is communicated enough eventually some of the populace will be swayed to that viewpoint and the proponent entity rises to power. Owning most of the media allows the Left to twist truth and change stories to their advantage. Following Socialist theory, leadership makes promises they cannot fulfill and incites revolution in the communities, such as the inner cities, most susceptible to their hollow promises. This is exactly how Adolf Hitler rose to power in Nazi Germany. His evil and destructive socialist empire did not last. His evil trail of death, horror, and destruction is well known. The design was to eliminate those that know history and in so doing history is erased. This has happened in many nations of the world and is no different from what is being attempted in our United States of America. Don't buy the lies or drink the cool aid of Democratic Socialists.

Roots of the Current Iteration

Barrack Obama and Hilary Clinton represent the current puppet leadership purveyors of Democratic Socialist ideology. Both were ardent disciples of community organizer and revolutionist Saul Alinsky. Hilary Clinton did her senior thesis, *"There Is Only the Fight . . . ": An Analysis of the Alinsky Model,* on her beloved mentor's methods. Barrack Obama cut his community organizing teeth using the model. These people never give up as they are intoxicated on the bait of Satan.

Depth and Organization of Democratic Socialism

The depth of Satan's plan is being implemented by the Deep State through those it controls. The American puppets were indoctrinated in Democratic Socialism by Marxist doctrine. Hilary Clinton's ideological thought comes from her mentor Saul Alinsky. Notice the following statement in Alinsky's book, *Rules for Radical*s: *"Lest we forget at least and over-the-shoulder acknowledgment to the very first radical: from all our legends, mythology, and history (and who is to know where mythology leaves off and history begins—or which is which), the first radical known to man who rebelled against the establishment and did it so effectively that he at least won his own* *kingdom—Lucifer."* Surprise, surprise – Satan, the first radical introducing to God's creation the original sin of rebellion and he has nurtured and grown it exponentially. Alinsky died before Barack Obama was able to mature and graduate from puppet school, although being raised by radicals steeped in Communist doctrine, young Barack was fertile soil with a huge hook already firmly seated. As a choice pick by the Deep State, Obama was assigned a master ideologist and trainer, Valerie Jarrett, to constantly assist, safeguard, and keep him on target throughout his ascent to power. The assault on the Republic has grown through many iterations and perpetrators, with different names and levels of growing violence but all tied to destruction of the Republic.

The Deep State Playbook

The ideology for Democratic Socialism is nothing more than Communism in a mask. The methodology of implementation is best laid out in the Cloward-Piven Strategy, devised by American students of Marxism, Richard Cloward and Frances Fox Piven. Their premise in moving a culture toward socialism and communism is orchestrated by starting a crisis so that the government can "solve" it. The four steps of the Cloward-Piven Strategy are:

1. Overload and break the systems
2. Have chaos ensue
3. Take control in the chaos

4. Implement socialism and communism through government force and control.

Application of Deep State Strategy in the United States

The implementation of Deep State strategy is accomplished by sucking the life from our Constitutional Republic and is contrary to the very constructs of our nation's founding fathers. These are knives in the heart of all truths the founding fathers deemed and held sacred. The implementation of the following tyrannous ideology will remove every freedom that we too often take for granted:

- **Healthcare**– Control healthcare. Premise: control the people.

- **Poverty** – Increase the poverty level. Premise: poor people are easier to control and will not fight back when the government provides everything for them to live.
- **Debt** – Increase the debt to an unsustainable level. Premise: Debt will require increased taxation, which will produce more poverty.
- **Gun Control** – Remove the ability of citizens to defend themselves from the government. Premise: create a police state.
- **Welfare** – Take control of every aspect of their lives (Food, Housing, and Income). Premise: dependence upon and fear of government.

- **Education** – Take control of schools. Premise: indoctrination of youth.
- **Religion** – Remove belief in God from government and schools. Premise: God is the enemy of the state and the source of liberty.
- **Class Warfare** – Divide people into the wealthy and the poor. Premise: cause more discontent and thus make it easier to tax the wealthy with the support of the poor.

Can you not see this playing out before our very eyes? The evil plan is cloaked and twisted by the Mainstream Media and funded by the vast resources of the Deep State. Do you really want to be devoid of liberty and justice as an imprisoned, impoverished, servant; ruled by a clown show of idiocy orchestrated by Satan's Deep State that even cares nothing for the henchmen that do their bidding? You know I'm speaking truth. If your answer is no to tyranny, you clearly understand the criticality of your vote in the November 2020 election and that every vote is a must. Don't be apathetic and found complicit in the fall of the Republic.

The Victor's Playbook

The Bible speaks with inerrancy into the events of the spiritual world such that it should not come as any surprise that we find ourselves embroiled in the age-old battle between good and evil. The battle is intensifying daily. We are given the Victor's playbook containing our instructions and prophetic events of the present and future which have or will occur. If we remain in or designated roles, we are assured to be among the victorious. Though we are given clues, only God the Father knows the timing and He operates in a vastly different time called eternal time (see 2 Peter 3:8). Bottomline is that we present and stand our ground, we war, and we win.

Where are We Now in God's Playbook?

Endless books and debate attempt to address where we are in God's plan. Though this inquisitive behavior is normal it is irrelevant to mission. Actually, everything one needs to know about the future is in the Old Testament book of Daniel. If one examines the prophetic in the book of

Revelation, they will see events that closely relate to where we are and things we are seeing. John the Apostle was exiled to the island of Patmos and wrote the vision he was given of the eschatological events leading to the second coming of Jesus Christ. Chapter 17 is Tribulation prophecy of the rise and fall of the "ecumenical world church" and Chapter 18 the destruction of a political system. They are both interesting and relevant. I am including verses from each that should allow you to easily see where we are in the unfolding drama.

Babylon #1

Revelation 17:1-2 reads *" And there came one of the seven angels which had the seven vials, and talked with me, Come hither; I will shew unto thee the judgement of the great whore that sitteth upon many waters: with whom the kings of the earth have committed fornication, and the inhabitants of the earth have been made drunk with the wine of her fornication."* This speaks of judgement of the great harlot of religious control over people and the fornication (idolatry) between this religious institution's leaders and the leadership of the world, from which evil Paul warns us in Romans 12:2 to be separated from. Can't you see the alignments forming internationally in this hour and the hypnotically drugged populace falling in step and marching straight into hell.

Babylon 2

After the events of Revelation 17, judgement of religious Babylon, we see God's horrendous judgements on the other Babylon, "Mystery Babylon", which is political Babylon. Revelation 18:1-5 paints a clear picture *"And after these things I saw another angel come down from heaven, having great power; and the earth was lightened with his glory. And he cried mightily with a strong voice, saying, Babylon the great is fallen, is fallen, and is become the habitation of devils, and the hold of every foul spirit, and a cage of every unclean and hateful bird. For all nations have drunk of the wine of the wrath of her fornication, and the kings of the earth have committed fornication with her, and the merchants of the earth are waxed rich through the abundance of her delicacies. And I heard another voice from heaven, saying, Come out of her, my people, that ye be not partakers of her sins, and that ye receive not of her plagues. For her sins have reached unto heaven, and God hath remembered her iniquities."*

If those complicit with rebelling against God, and leading others with them, don't render witness of the coming judgements while on earth, they will surely see their legacy from the pit of Hell.

Back to November 2020

Regardless of your level of understanding, you either believe or disbelieve the resolve of our founding fathers. They believed in a Constitutional Republic as distinguished from a pure Democracy. History has shown the latter to result in abject failure. The United States, though not perfect, has resulted in the best model to date for a free and thriving nation. Do you really want to throw this out and become enslaved to an elite ruling class? If you are so deceived that you can't readily or upon reflection see what is unfolding before your very eyes, then no amount of rhetoric will help you see the truth.

Some Trusted Supporting Information

Even without presenting the lefts playbook, if one were to fully engage their brain it would be obvious that the cites in chaos have Democratic Left leadership. Some are even comparing the total chaos and anarchy of Seattle and Portland with Kristallnacht in 1938 Nazi Germany. I trust the opinions and factual data from the Heritage Foundation, a conservative and legitimate think-tank in Washington DC focused on public policy. It goes without saying that my understanding of truth comes from the Bible and that which Holy Spirit shows me, but I decided to examine a few articles from the Heritage Foundation to justify my thought processes with regard to the current political state of the Nation. I share some excerpts from the following articles:

The Agenda of Black Lives Matter is Far Different From the Slogan, Mike Gonzalez & Andrew Olivastro, July 3, 2020,
https://www.heritage.org/progressivism/commentary/the-agenda-black-lives-matter-far-different-the-slogan

Just ask BLM leaders Alicia Garza, Patrisse Cullors and Opal Tometi. In a revealing 2015 interview, Cullors said, "Myself and Alicia in particular are trained organizers. We are trained Marxists."

The group's radical Marxist agenda would supplant the basic building block of society—the family—with the state and destroy the economic system that has lifted more people from poverty than any other.

A partner organization, the Movement for Black Lives, or M4BL, calls for abolishing all police and all prisons. It also calls for a "progressive restructuring of tax codes at the local, state and federal levels to ensure a radical and sustainable redistribution of wealth."

Another M4BL demand is "the retroactive decriminalization, immediate release and record expungement of all drug-related offenses and prostitution and reparations for the devastating impact of the 'war on drugs' and criminalization of prostitution."

Nations Values Under Attack-We Must Do This to Stop the Left's Socialist Agenda , Kay C. James July 3, 2020

https://www.heritage.org/civil-society/commentary/nations-values-under-attack-we-must-do-stop-the-lefts-socialist-agenda

Our country is under attack from radical leftists. Mobs rampage through our streets, monuments are being destroyed, and the very law and order that ensures our communities' peace and security is being undermined...In far too many instances, those bent on destruction have hijacked protests, creating violence and division and ultimately attacking the very foundation of our nation. For them, it's not about resolving race issues; it's about using racial discontent to forward their anarchist agenda.

One such group is Antifa. While it is widely recognized as a far-left fringe group, another organization—just as radical—has managed to drape itself in more mainstream clothes, gaining significant support with the public, politicians and the business community. While Americans of every color agree with the sentiment that black lives matter, Black Lives Matter (BLM) the organization actually advocates an agenda that is completely out of step with American values. Groups like Antifa and the BLM organization want to impose an ideology on America that would only bring greater poverty, a loss of freedom, destruction to churches and civil society, and violent law enforcement tactics to enforce compliance—exactly what we've seen in places like Venezuela, Cuba and North Korea.

Finally, we must combat the Marxist agenda. This agenda has wrought destruction on nations for generations. It expands government control and takes every opportunity to limit freedom, and it must not take root in the United States.

The most desperate communities in America have been run by the left for a generation or more. We've seen what that leadership has brought: generational poverty, fatherless families, worse educational outcomes, more disparity and higher crime rates. Lurching even further left would be even more disastrous.

Conservatives have always had the policies that can help solve many of the difficult issues that Americans face. We know how to create jobs, end poverty, provide better access to health care, improve education and strengthen families better than anyone. And our fundamental belief in the inherent dignity of every human being can help bring about the healing our nation so desperately needs.

Defend U.S. Statues and Monuments: Here's What the Mobs Really Want to Destroy Jun 30th, 2020 Nile Gaediner, Ph.D. & Joseph Loconte, Ph.D.)

(https://www.heritage.org/civil-society/commentary/defend-us-statues-and-monuments-heres-what-the-mobs-really-want-destroy

The radical left has hijacked debate over America's monuments to wage a cultural war. Their goal: to deny the moral legitimacy of our democratic republic….Violent attacks on statues and memorials aren't mere vandalism. They are an assault on the United States itself and the values upon which this great nation stands. We should all stand united as Americans in the defense *of our heritage, culture and the rule of law...In America, as in Great Britain, we have built statues to memorialize individuals and events representing some of the noblest moments in our civilization. Such artwork helps us to remember and defend our highest political, moral and religious ideals. The mob violence directed against it is an assault on civilization itself...Prime Minister Boris Johnson and French President Emmanuel Macron have taken a strong stand against the far Left's attempts to bring down statues representing their nations' cultural heritage...Johnson condemned the attacks on Churchill, and other monuments declaring that "the statue of Winston Churchill in Parliament Square is a permanent reminder of his achievement in saving this country—and the whole of Europe—from a fascist and racist tyranny. It is absurd and shameful that this national monument should today be at risk of attack by violent protestors. "The United States is the leader of the free world. No nation in history has done more to defend the principles of liberty and freedom. America's very foundations today are under attack from left-wing anarchists who seek to sow fear, disorder, violence and hatred. We cannot allow the forces of anarchy to replace the rule of law. They must not be allowed to win.*

Mob Rule Imperils Western Civilization. Now's the Time for Courage and Leadership Jun 29th, 2020 Jarrett Simpson
https://www.heritage.org/civil-society/commentary/mob-rule-imperils-western-civilization-nows-the-time-courage-and

As I explained in my book, "The War on History: The Conspiracy to Rewrite America's Past," the attacks on our shared history go beyond any individual or statue...What's in peril now is not just the reputation of Christopher Columbus, the merits of the Founding Fathers, or the legacy of the Civil War. It's something much broader and deeper...What's being threatened is the long history of ideas and institutions created and developed in the West...The United States, of course, has been the prime target of radicals, because—whether we chose this role or not—it is the pinnacle of Western *prosperity and strength…In an address at Bristol University in 1938, the British prime minister-to-be warned that civilization itself was under attack, that it would be tested, and that it would survive only if free people drew on their strength and courage to defend it…In words striking in the face of our challenges today, Churchill said: "Civilization will not last, freedom will not survive, peace will not be kept, unless a very large majority of mankind unite together to defend them and show themselves possessed of a constabulary power before which barbaric and atavistic forces will stand in awe."…Will we, like generations before us, answer the call to defend our way of life? Will it be the generation that grew up at the "end of history"—after the Nazi menace was crushed by the arsenal of democracy, the USSR's evil empire collapsed, and free people stood triumphant—that will cast our hard-won victories aside in an effort to purge our imperfect past?...In an era of mob rule— where the very basis of American and Western civilization is being questioned and attacked from within, and when rising superpowers like communist China that stand in opposition to everything we represent are on the march—it is essential that free people resist the impulses leading to our self-immolation...Now we are again being called upon to mount a defense of our way of life. We have a great deal to lose and much at stake, because what's at stake are not just statues and stone, but the freedom of millions alive today and the many more yet unborn.*

Incriminating Evidence from BLM Leader

From Fox News, Martha MacCallum on 'The Story.' June 24, 2020, https://video.foxnews.com/v/6167027878001#sp=show-clips,

I present evidence from Black Lives Matter Greater New York Chair, Hawk Newsome on the movement's goals: "I said," Newsome told the host, "if this country doesn't give us what we want, then we will burn down this system and replace it. All right? And I could be speaking ... figuratively. I could be speaking literally. It's a matter of interpretation"...At the conclusion of the interview, Newsome told MacCallum, "I just want black liberation and black sovereignty, by any means necessary.

Critical Race Theory

Critical race theory is a theoretical framework, rooted in Marxism, that posits individuals as oppressed or oppressor based on their skin color. So, what is meant by the terms Socialism- Marxism- Communism? Karl Marx, the father of communism, was outraged by the growing gap between rich and poor. He saw capitalism as an outmoded economic system that exploited workers, which would eventually rise against the rich because the poor were so unfairly treated. Marx thought that the economic system of Communism should and would replace capitalism. Communism, based on the principles and ideology of Marxism, was meant to correct what Marx saw as problems caused by capitalism.

Ideology of the Left

Communism allows for no private ownership of property. Marx believed that private ownership encouraged greed. Property should be shared, and the people should ultimately control the economy. The government should exercise the control in the name of the people, during transition between capitalism and communism. The goals are to eliminate the gap between rich and poor and to bring economic equality.

These ideas are insanity which never worked and never will.

Socialism, like communism, calls for putting the major means of production in the hands of the people, either directly or through the government. Socialism also believes that wealth and income should be shared more equally among people. Socialists differ from communists in that they do not believe that the workers will overthrow capitalists suddenly and violently. Socialism does not believe in the elimination of all private property. Their main goal is to narrow, not totally eliminate, the gap between the rich and the poor. Socialists believe that it is the responsibility of government to redistribute wealth to make society fairer and just. Does this agenda sound familiar?

The theories are a bit confusing, but none work because they all lead to shared poverty with a leadership that prospers. Back in the day when our government was concerned about these destructive issues, I as a Florida high school student was required to take a state mandated six-week course entitled "Americanism vs Communism." I don't recall much other than it revealed the evil of Communism, which I still think is important. It was deemed important from 1961-1983 by my state as we had Communism 90 miles off our shore in Cuba.

The theory of the left draws from the theoretical construct of Marxism, but leaders can't consummate theory because retention of their wealth, power, and the benefits/delicacies they enjoy on the back of the taxpayer would cease to exist. Can you imagine leadership in the U.S. House or Senate using the health insurance that has been thrust on the public or serving the nation on an appropriate salary, with term limits and a 401K plan for that term? Many of those on the right also have forgotten their Constitutional roots and are enjoying and unwilling to give up their place at the golden trough.

Compassionate Capitalism and the Republic

The compassionate capitalism of a Republic is the only form of government that has proven workable. Granted there are those that can't fend for themselves, via disability, and they should be cared for (which was once a responsibility supported by the church to which we as the body of Christ should be adjudged negligent) but the majority of those of non-capitalist persuasion are guilty of being lazy and of the belief that providing entitlement is the responsibility of those that produce within the economy and those should therefore support the unsustainable government folly of the Left. We have for the most part elected a National Congress and Senate complicit with allowing the degradation of our culture because they are consumed with power and greed. I will say that many started with good intentions, but the deep state found a way to put an inescapable hook within them and Satan became victor and their master.

The great project in freedom of our forefathers, with Constitutional checks and balances, has reached an inescapable junction. The Left has pushed the envelope too far this time with an ugly hatred that is not going away easily and has brought lawlessness and anarchy upon our Nation. Many on the Right have cowardly not given support to the POTUS who has had to carry the entire burden. President Trump has a backbone of steel and the support of Almighty God, both of which have enabled him to stand and govern justly with incredible success through constant ugly and unfounded efforts at his destruction

Who knows what the next move from the Left will be? You can be assured that they will keep hurling insanity to make the POTUS look bad. They have been on a ridiculous and fruitless witch hunt from the day the sitting President was elected. Prior to his election the Democrats illegally colluded to ensure their victory if it were to become jeopardized as they secured the infamous Dossier compiled by Christopher Steele and paid for by Hillary Clinton and the Democratic National Committee (DNC). The dossier contained allegations of misconduct, conspiracy and cooperation between candidate Donald Trump and Russia. The document presented no substantial evidence.

Failure After Failure – It Needs to End

Attempt after attempt to destroy the POTUS have yielded nothing. The Democrats pinned their hope on an extensive investigation by Robert Mueller, then on an impeachment attempt. These major initiatives and smaller initiatives interspersed throughout the President's term have all fallen short of their goals. How the Left justifies the extremely huge and continuous expenditures of taxpayer dollars with the attenuating destruction of the nation and economy, fruitless while their primary work is ignored, is beyond my understanding. I will also say that far too many Republicans are sipping the cool aid, and having been enslaved by power, greed, and the compromise of character that the deep state insidiously tempts and so effectively orchestrates, have themselves become complicit in corruption.

A Modern Day Cyrus

My thought is that the POTUS is truly sent by God to insure America's part in His providential purpose. He is like a Cyrus, the ancient King of Persia that allowed the captive Israelites to return to their homeland and rebuild Jerusalem. Donald

Trump has not backed down and has obtained incredible results despite all that has been done to bring his demise. Many Christian prophets have prophesied that he will have a second term. Prophecy today is usually conditional, which means you and I must do our part, and in this instance cast a ballot.

I also believe that Covid19 was designed by the elite of Satan's followers to cause destruction and gain submission of good God-fearing people. The development of a vaccine will most likely carry a microchip in the name of tracking the disease, but with real purpose of controlling citizens worldwide.

You can write me off as a crazy far-right proponent of conspiracy theory or you can realize that I am a patriot that hears from God. I hope you take this seriously and act accordingly. The consequences of a wrong decision or apathy in this election could throw our nation into a tailspin from which another civil war may be the only way to recover. The wrong decision will make you captive to some very ugly enslavement or death. In so many ways the hope of most of the world rests on your correct decision.

CHAPTER 7

THE AWAKENING MUST HAPPEN

There is a Better Option

As I said in the last chapter, the left has pushed the envelope too far and either result in the November 3, 2020 Presidential election is going to come with pain and issues that can't be resolved overnight.

If the Democrat candidate prevails, I believe the lawlessness and anarchy of a portion of the public will be almost impossible to quell in a manner that the nation can return to some degree of normalcy. I am not an economist, but the logical mind can conclude that a socialist agenda will cause hyperinflation, unbearable taxation and this will lead to an inevitable implosion of the economy.

If the Republican candidate prevails, I believe Donald Trump's abilities and skills will build a strong economy which will calm some of the anarchy and rebellion. I believe that the nation will see the wickedness of some of the deep state and its puppet leaders revealed to such a depth that it can no longer be hidden and tolerated by the decent law-abiding citizens of the nation. The Supreme Court will also shift toward ideology of the Constitutional Republic. The respite will last a few years as the evil core of the Deep State replicates new henchmen to again push the nation until it is at the precipice of destruction.

These are imperfect models from the minds of men. The American experiment in a constitutional republic had favor from its beginning because its very foundation was in God. The founding fathers always sought Him before taking action. Their dependence upon Him is reflected not only in the foundational documents but in the invocation of His name at assembly.

Ideology of the Left Will Never Work

The current socialist elements of society are adamant about destroying any trace of God and the history of the Nation. This is a terrible step in the wrong direction. The

Democratic leadership of the United States, in condoning anarchy and rebellion to attain their goals, seem to lack the mental acuity to realize their plans will fail and bring destruction. The Left seem clueless, much like a deer caught in the headlights, to the results of serving their evil masters and seemingly lack the wisdom to comprehend that their actions lead to totalitarianism. George Orwell, pen name of socialist Eric Arthur Blair, wrote a novel published in 1949 entitled <u>Nineteen Eighty-Four</u>. The novel is a warning of the serious danger totalitarianism poses to society. As a socialist he believed strongly in the potential of rebellion to cause advances in society, but he witnessed that such rebellions often go wrong and develop into totalitarian rule.

The Real Solution - Ecclesia

The only viable solution to our nation's problems and those of all nations is Kingdom Culture and establishment of the King's Ecclesia. The King is Jesus Christ, to whom Almighty God gave the nations as His inheritance. Ecclesia is the correct word for what was incorrectly translated as church. The two have almost totally different meanings. Church means assembly. Ecclesia means a ruling, voting, corporate body to exercise Christ's authority on earth through permitting or forbidding on the earth. For people who live the culture of the Kingdom, Ecclesia becomes possible.

The first century apostles were given blueprints and mandates from Jesus. After the Ascension of Jesus, the promised Holy Spirit came upon them. They were emboldened and empowered to turn their world upside down, which they did until Rome conquered their known world. Ecclesia was lost and only in our era has it been rediscovered. I'm sure that for many, even in the church, this is foreign to your knowledge and thought processes, but is very real. We are on the precipice of a new Pentecost. Many believe this new Pentecost arrived during the celebration of the event this year, commemorating when the apostles and disciples of Jesus experienced the first Pentecost, where Holy Spirit came upon them and activated/empowered/emboldened them to establish Ecclesia.

I am sure, unless you are a millennial, you know the acceleration of the world in which we exist. If you are a baby-boomer or have spoken seriously with one about our youth, you can reflect, compare, and contrast such that you will see it as well, the darkness that has moved in. If you read your Bible, converse with the Lord and be led by Holy Spirit, you will understand the times. Satan's time is getting very short and his plan has accelerated. Believers worldwide have been persecuted and it will get worse.

But God... He continues to extend His grace and I sometimes think He must personally orchestrate a few things that we miss. Regardless, the truth is that He expects you and me to accomplish His purposes on the earth. We have been given the keys, the tools and the mandate. I realize that eternity runs on a much different timeclock than we do. In light of all that is transpiring today, I would think His patience must be wearing thin.

Everything that I am hearing and seeing prophetically lets me know that this decade of the 2020's is the most important to date. It is a decade of reformation, harvest and supernatural intervention. I am sure that by now I have provided something to stimulate thought and hopefully action. I do know where I will be going when I graduate from the earthly battle, but I know I'm not through yet. I will do all things that I am destined by God to do through Christ, being strengthened by the Dunamis power of Holy Spirit dwelling in and manifesting through me.

Providential Purpose

God's favor is on my native United States because He has given a providential purpose to her as a fathering nation to the world. The United States has shed blood for, given of its abundance, and spread the Gospel of Jesus Christ globally. She is in need of a transfusion to get through this impasse in which we find ourselves spiritually and physically. I had a prophetic vision during worship at Freedom House, Jacksonville, Florida, June 21, 2020: *I saw the earth in global form and red bands were moving as if tracking an airplane circling the* globe. As I watch they were moving across Africa and Europe away from the Americas. Then from pole to pole blue bands encircle the globe outside the red ones, sort of a wheel within a wheel. Then I saw African people, then Middle East people, then Europe, Asia, Australia, and Island nations. All were seeking the Light and the Glory hovering over Jerusalem.

I asked Holy Spirit what this meant and where were North and South America? This is His response: The red is streams of Christ's blood washing and empowering those that will receive. It is the power that moves the blue wheel. The blue wheel is the dominion and perpetuity of His government. The Americas are not in it as they need a transfusion. They will repent, reform and *move through a Kairos Window and again take their providential purpose/leadership role in the Nations. The plagues will vanish when the nations repent – that is Biblical as it has always been. Look up Man of God.*

My Decree
We desperately need strong leadership that will uplift the nation, not destroy it. *I decree that it will happen through the reelection of Donald Trump as POTUS. I decree that the United States will heal and retake her place in her providential purpose destined by God.*

A New Pentecost
The new Pentecost that many in the body of Christ are seeing began May 31, 2020, on the celebration of the original Pentecost when Holy Spirit arrived as Jesus

promised. This is exciting to me because it definitively signals that God is with us in this dark time to protect His own and assure His providential purpose. We will have to fight, but we win! This fresh infusion of Holy Spirit Dunamis Power will increase. We are in God's hand and as long as we are submitted to Him we can rest in the secret place of the Most High protected and refreshed from the battle.

The Father Laughs

Psalm 2, a co-favorite of mine along with 91, is prophetic in that it is about the second coming of Jesus Christ, more than it was about King David. It also speaks very accurately to what we are seeing today. "Why are the nations in an uproar and the peoples devising a vain thing? The kings of the earth take their stand and the rulers take counsel together against the Lord and against His Anointed, saying, 'Let us tear their fetters apart and cast away their cords from us!'" (Psalm 2:1-3). Is this not happening worldwide and more specifically in our nation as rebellion rails against God and wears away at the fetters of moral restraint? "He who sits in the heavens laughs, the Lord scoffs at them. Then He will speak to them in His anger and terrify them in His fury" (Psalm 2:4-5). God sees it all and laughs at the foolishness of those in full revolt. They seem to not know or even care that God's judgments extend to them. Why does the Lord delay His full judgment? The Lord waits for us, His Ecclesia. For while the world shall demand, and receive, the reign of Hell, the goal of the praying Ecclesia is for the reign of Heaven. **All of God's prophecies shall be fulfilled: those concerning evil as well as those concerning righteousness.** The Lord will have a "Bride without spot or wrinkle" and a "Kingdom" devoid of wickedness. The Body of Christ, His Ecclesia, will be transformed just as every other prophecy will be fulfilled before the Lord's return. Then in the midst of what is going on the Father says to the son "Ask of Me and I will give You the nations as Your inheritance, and the uttermost parts of the earth as Your possession" (Psalm 2:8 Amplified Version).

Repent – The Kingdom of Heaven is at Hand

It is time to repent and stand firm in our faith. Ephesians 2:6 tells us that we are "seated with Him in the heavenly places." As such we should rejoice, even in light of seeing our world unravel. God has us in His hand, has given us Kingdom keys and sharpened swords, Holy Spirit within us and angelic armies to assist. If you stand in faith you have all these and the promise of eternity. I can attest to this having done things and been places that would cause some to question my sanity. When I go to my beloved Africa I always see, miracles, signs, and wonders, as well as The Light and The Glory pouring out on a people desperate for God. I believe and decree that these things will manifest again in my native United States of America.

God is Speaking Volumes in These Days

God is speaking to those with ears to hear. He is asking if you will be one of His Holy Remnant. Will you set aside things and people that you have made "golden calves" and seek Him? God is once again shaking everything that can be shaken. Will you seek the King of Glory and escape the bondage of consumerism, religion, and all other things that would take your eyes off Jesus. This shaking is not gentle because He needs your attention NOW.

Comply with the King's edict and watch a tsunami of His Glory fill you and empower you to shake nations in His Name. As you sit in heavenly places, you will laugh with Him at the chaos that was once fearful to you. I am interceding for you to join the ranks. All of creation is groaning for the manifest presence of the Sons of God. Your joining the ranks is what the Gospel is all about.

November 3, 2020

With regard to November 3, 2020 it will be your decision if you vote. I am a temporary resident sent on a mission by the King and a voice crying out to a demonic sea of evil trying to get a buoy to those that are missing the big picture.

The sea is physical but is really more spiritual. The physical is two candidates with totally different agendas and perspective. Only God can heal the nation, so the question becomes do you choose a constitutional republic and becoming healthy again or do you choose a tailspin of violence, destruction, pain and poverty of socialist leadership? This is the most important decision we have ever had to make as a nation. I am praying and believing that we will make the correct decision.

Vision of Victory

The Lord has given me prophetic gifting, though not my primary ministry gift, this seer type gifting is very useful and exciting.

On July 16, 2020 I had a vision, which I include here because it correlates with my decree and belief in God's intervention regardless of the evil surrounding the coming election. *As we were praying, I saw the four of us sharpening swords for battle. As we were so doing angels walked down our stairs, four of which were carrying mantles. They presented before us and the spokesman declared: " I am here on orders of the Most High God to mantle you. He instructed me to tell you that He has noticed faithfulness and effectiveness in your sacrifice and intercession and that it is time to move you to a higher level and purpose and I am delivering the mantles. The Holy One said that you would know what to do because you hear His voice." The angels placed the mantles upon our shoulders, and I saw a war being waged. It was a fierce battle between soldiers arrayed in red and soldiers arrayed in blue. Then it abruptly ended and all I saw was dust and smoke, but suddenly a troop of soldiers emerged marching in purple array carrying gold swords and shields. They marched in formation executing a pass and review. As they approached the reviewing stand and rendered salute to the leader,* **I recognized that leader to be President Donald Trump.**

My prophetic vision is rather obvious, and I believe President Donald Trump will have a second term, but God works through us and it is not the time to be apathetic. We are engaged in a war and you must do your part if you want to keep your freedom.

The Truth Will Set You Free

I realize that I have perhaps been rather harsh, but someone must speak the truth. Only the truth will set you free and He alone, the Spirit of truth, can truly give you liberty and life abundant. Seek the King of Kings and live. I speak the truth as well as bless you in Jesus name.

COME KINGDOM OF GOD – WILL OF GOD HAPPEN IN MY NATION AND IN THE NATIONS AROUND THE WORLD!

EPILOGUE

I am going to publish this work as soon as possible. We are in a very fluid and highly combustible time. This epic battle in which we find ourselves is very fluid, combustible and changes daily. I ask you to be forgiving for lack of perfection, but time is of the essence and I must publish soon. If my book causes only a few to see the light, then it is well worth my effort.

Just today, 8 August 2020, I listened to President Trump's broadcast and signing of Executive Orders for the citizenry to provide relief during the Covid-19 crisis. President Trump made this call to assist the citizens hurt by Deep State actions through their puppet lawmakers to bring destruction upon himself and our fellow Americans. The US House and Senate could not reach an agreement because of allocation amounts, but there was an extremely ominous dark effort by the Democratic House to package within their bill provisions to steal the Presidency through mail balloting and harvesting of ballets.

Just today, 8 August 2020, at Freedom House Jacksonville, I attended and participated the most powerful Holy Spirit fired Apostolic/Prophetic Conference I have ever experienced. It will take a while to unpack all the revelation I received. Everything is being shaken and the heat rises each day. I must give my best shot now, as I don't have the luxury of waiting any longer. At best my treatise will be available sixty days prior to election.

Evil will not succumb easily, and it is time to fight for this great nation and the freedom we enjoy. We owe it to those that went before us as well as our children such that they can experience freedom too. Cast a wise ballot on or before November 3, 2020.

OTHER BOOKS BY GUY DIFFENBAUGH

Purpose in the Kings Call

Africa Chronicles I

Great Faith: *The Key to 2019 & The Coming Move Of God*

Jacksonville: *The Tip of the Spear*

www.ingramcontent.com/pod-product-compliance
Lightning Source LLC
Chambersburg PA
CBHW022357040426
42450CB00005B/228